GREAT BASEBALL
BY MARTY GITLIN

DEBATES

GREAT
SPORTS
DEBATES

SportsZone
An Imprint of Abdo Publishing | abdopublishing.com

ABDOPUBLISHING.COM

Published by Abdo Publishing, a division of ABDO, PO Box 398166, Minneapolis, Minnesota 55439. Copyright © 2019 by Abdo Consulting Group, Inc. International copyrights reserved in all countries. No part of this book may be reproduced in any form without written permission from the publisher. SportsZone™ is a trademark and logo of Abdo Publishing.

Printed in the United States of America, North Mankato, Minnesota
032018
092018

THIS BOOK CONTAINS RECYCLED MATERIALS

Cover Photos: Amy Sancetta/AP Images, right, left
Interior Photos: Frank Jansky/Icon Sportswire/AP Images, 4–5; Elaine Thompson/AP Images, 6; Joshua Sarner/Icon Sportswire/AP Images, 8, 14–15; Richard Drew/AP Images, 11; Bill Wippert/AP Images, 12–13; Chris O'Meara/AP Images, 16; Kevin Abele/Icon Sportswire/AP Images, 18; AP Images, 20–21, 26; Lenny Ignelzi/AP Images, 22; New York Times Co./Archive Photos/Getty Images, 23; Tony Gutierrez/AP Images, 24; Harry Harris/AP Images, 28–29; Kathy Willens/AP Images, 31, 44–45; John Cordes/Icon Sportswire/AP Images, 32; Tony Tomsic/AP Images, 34–35; Bain News Service/Library of Congress, 36; Leon Algee/AP Images, 38–39; Bill Kostroun/AP Images, 41; Craig Fujii/AP Images, 42; Tim Clayton/Corbis Sport/Getty Images, 45

Editor: Patrick Donnelly
Series Designer: Laura Polzin

Library of Congress Control Number: 2017961928

Publisher's Cataloging-in-Publication Data

Names: Gitlin, Marty, author.
Title: Great baseball debates / by Marty Gitlin.
Description: Minneapolis, Minnesota : Abdo Publishing, 2019. | Series: Great sports debates | Includes online resources and index.
Identifiers: ISBN 9781532114410 (lib.bdg.) | ISBN 9781532154249 (ebook)
Subjects: LCSH: Baseball players--Juvenile literature. | Baseball--Records--United States--Juvenile literature. | Sports--History--Juvenile literature. | Debates and debating--Juvenile literature.
Classification: DDC 796.357--dc23

TABLE OF CONTENTS

CHAPTER 1
A SNAIL'S PACE 4

CHAPTER 2
DUMP THE UMP? 14

CHAPTER 3
COMPARING ERAS 20

CHAPTER 4
THE DH DIFFERENCE 28

CHAPTER 5
WHO BELONGS IN THE HALL? 34

FURTHER DISCUSSION 44		**MORE INFORMATION** 47	
GLOSSARY 46		**INDEX** 48	
ONLINE RESOURCES 47		**ABOUT THE AUTHOR** 48	

A pitcher reads his catcher's signals to know which type of pitch he should throw.

CHAPTER ONE

A SNAIL'S PACE

The pitcher steps off the mound. He takes off his glove and rubs the baseball between his bare hands. He returns to the mound and peers at the catcher, who is flashing signs. The catcher puts down one finger and wiggles it to his left. That means he wants a fastball inside.

The pitcher shakes his head. He'd rather throw a curveball outside. The catcher shows three fingers, calling for a slider. The pitcher shakes him off again.

Now the hitter becomes impatient. He steps out of the batter's box. He adjusts his batting gloves. He spits on the ground. He taps both cleats with his bat to clear away any dirt they might have accumulated in the previous 30 seconds.

Batters sometimes ask the umpire for a timeout if they think a pitcher is taking too long on the mound.

He wiggles his helmet back down on his head. Then he finally steps back into the box.

The catcher puts down two fingers. That means he wants a curveball. He and the pitcher are finally on the same page.

But now the pitcher throws the ball to first base to keep the runner close. By the time he finally throws the ball to the plate, more than a minute has passed since his last pitch.

This scene plays out multiple times in every Major League Baseball (MLB) game. Many fans don't mind it. They like that baseball is the only major American sport without a clock. But others hate it. Baseball is simply too slow for them. That has led to a debate. Should MLB find ways to speed up the game, or should it maintain its leisurely pace?

The pace of play used to be no problem. The average game lasted approximately 2 hours in 1944. But it has been steadily rising. The average reached 2:30 in 1959. It hit 3 hours for the first time in 2014. It reached 3:05 in 2017. Yet in some respects, baseball remains as popular as ever. The average crowd at a major league game topped 30,000 in 2017. National TV ratings have risen. So why try to speed things up?

One reason is that research shows baseball is turning off younger fans. Those fans represent its future popularity. And younger fans like sports with more action and less downtime. They tend to embrace football and basketball, or extreme sports and video games.

What is slowing down the average baseball game? It's not just the pitcher shaking off signs from the catcher. It goes beyond the batter stepping out of the box. It's more than catchers visiting the mound to talk to pitchers.

One of the biggest issues is pitching changes. Starting pitchers rarely throw complete games these days. Managers often use multiple relief pitchers to get through the latter innings of a game. They might bring in a left-hander to face one left-handed batter. Then they might summon a right-hander to face a right-handed batter. The setup man pitches the eighth inning. Then the closer comes on in the ninth.

All of that gives radio and TV stations time for commercials. It allows fans a chance to visit the concession stand for another hot dog and soda. But it slows the game to a crawl.

MLB officials have stated that they want to speed up the game. They just haven't figured out how. They have tried to cut down on the time between innings. Yet game times keep getting longer.

So what steps can be taken to shorten games? One common suggestion has been setting a time limit between pitches.

Visits to the mound by coaches and catchers can make a game drag.

THE WORST OFFENDER

When former Texas Rangers and Cleveland Indians first baseman Mike Hargrove came to bat, he turned heads with his prolonged routine between every pitch. Hargrove would step out of the batter's box. Then he'd paw at the dirt with his foot, tap his cleats with his bat, adjust his batting glove, tug on his belt, and rub his nose. If he didn't put the next pitch in play, it would start all over again. It's no wonder he was nicknamed "the Human Rain Delay."

Should a pitcher be given just 20 seconds to throw the ball? A 20-second clock has been adopted in the minor leagues. It has sped up the game by an average of approximately 12 minutes.

Some believe that is unfair to the pitcher. He has a lot to think about. He has to hold runners close to their bases. He has to think about what type of pitch would work best against a certain hitter. And he has to think about where he will throw the ball if the batter hits it to him.

Can MLB limit the number of pitching changes a manager can make? Most believe that would weaken his ability to win games. It would also have a major effect on the strategy of the sport.

MLB has taken steps to make its replay system more efficient.

MLB has experimented with a pitch clock in the minor leagues.

And what about replay challenges? They've also slowed the game down. Umpires sometimes take two or three minutes to learn if they got a call right. But is it not important to ensure the correct call?

What can be done to speed up the game without ruining it? That question has been asked for many years. And nobody seems to have a good answer.

Batters and umpires often have disagreements over ball/strike calls.

CHAPTER TWO

DUMP THE UMP?

The pitcher hurls a slider toward the plate. It looks like it's headed toward the strike zone. But it darts suddenly to the right. The batter thinks it's a ball and doesn't swing.

"Strike one!" yells the umpire as he jerks his arm into the air. The batter turns and has a few harsh words for the umpire.

The pitcher winds up and fires a fastball. It looks like it catches the inside corner for a strike. "Ball one!" Now it is the pitcher's turn to be unhappy. He glares at the umpire.

It's a baseball tradition. Pitchers and hitters have been getting angry at home plate umpires since the 1800s. The umps have a tough job. They have to interpret the strike zone

Calling balls and strikes is one of the most difficult jobs in sports.

on every pitch. Major league pitchers throw baseballs with late movement. The balls dart and plunge into and out of the strike zone in a fraction of a second. Many pitches cross home plate on the border of the strike zone. Hitters and pitchers both want that call to go their way. Someone is going to come away upset with the result.

There might be a solution. Could the job of calling balls and strikes be handled by a computer or robot? No umpire would lose his job. There would still be a need to call runners safe or out at the plate and to rule whether a batted ball is fair or foul. But technology exists that can call balls and strikes more accurately. Should it be used in MLB?

Traditionalists argue against it. They offer that the human element must remain in the game. They believe imperfections are part of baseball and think arguments between players and umpires make the game more fun. But many say balls and strikes should not be judgment calls. Where a pitch crosses the plate does not change. They want MLB to take all possible steps to get calls right. They claim that computers or robots would be more precise. And they are probably right.

First, however, umpires would have to agree where the strike zone is. It's supposed to be over home plate, extending from the batter's knees to the letters on the front of his uniform. But how an umpire calls the strike zone often varies from what's outlined in the rule book. A few umpires call higher pitches strikes. Many others call lower pitches strikes. Some lean over

THE ART OF FRAMING

Sometimes an umpire can be convinced to call a strike on a pitch that didn't cross the plate. It often happens when a catcher subtly turns his glove toward the strike zone after catching pitches out of the zone. The practice is called "framing," and if it's done well, a catcher can use it to steal a couple of extra strikes per game.

the inside or outside corner of the plate. Then they have a hard time seeing pitches on the opposite side of the plate.

How would it change baseball if a computer umpire began calling strikes according to the rule book? Pitchers and batters would probably get used to it. Should umpires simply be told to adjust their strike zones themselves?

Can we trust computers to make the perfect call on every pitch to every batter? And would removing the human element be good for baseball?

The strike zone is defined in the rule book, but umpires don't all call it the same way.

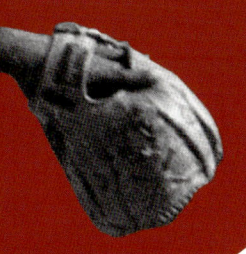

Bob Gibson of the St. Louis Cardinals helped make 1968 "the Year of the Pitcher."

CHAPTER THREE

COMPARING ERAS

The year was 1910. Babe Ruth was just a teenager growing up in Baltimore. Baseballs were a bit softer than the ones used today. It took a mighty wallop for a major league batter to hit a ball over the fence. The most anyone slugged that year was 10.

Fast forward to 1927. The dead-ball era was over. Ruth set a record by slamming 60 home runs that year. Baseball had been changed forever.

Move on to 1968. It was known as the Year of the Pitcher. St. Louis Cardinals right-hander Bob Gibson dominated the National League. He posted a 1.12 earned-run average (ERA) that season. That means he gave up approximately one run per nine innings. So MLB lowered the mound in every ballpark the next season, hoping hitters would have a better chance.

Jump ahead to 2001. Many players were suspected to be taking performance-enhancing drugs (PEDs) to gain power. San Francisco Giants slugger Barry Bonds shattered the single-season home run record by smashing 73. Balls were flying over fences in ridiculous numbers.

Barry Bonds, *right*, watches one of his 73 home runs in 2001.

Babe Ruth paved the way for today's home run sluggers.

Every baseball era was different. And it's not just about statistics. Players once traveled by train to cities no farther west than the Mississippi River. Now they travel by plane throughout North America. Pitchers have perfected pitches that move unlike anything seen by batters of previous generations. Outfielders' gloves are much bigger, helping them turn long fly

Is it fair to compare modern stars such as Mike Trout (27) to Willie Mays and other all-time greats from different eras?

balls into outs. Big money has motivated players to stay in great shape all year. It seems impossible to compare different eras of the sport. But can we compare players from those eras?

Los Angeles Angels center fielder Mike Trout has reminded some of the great Willie Mays. One could argue that Mays faced far better starting pitchers in the 1950s and 1960s. MLB had fewer teams, so the outstanding pitching wasn't spread so thin. But Trout is seeing split-fingered fastballs and other pitches that weren't thrown in Mays's era. And today's pitchers are athletes who are better trained and are selected from a broader pool of talent.

What about Los Angeles Dodgers left-handers Sandy Koufax and Clayton Kershaw? Koufax was in his prime in the 1960s. He made batters swing and miss in an era when they took pride in making contact. Kershaw pitches in modern times, when hitters swing for the fences. Many of them approach an at-bat with the idea that a strikeout is no worse than any other kind of out. It was once shameful for a player to strike out 100 times in a season. Now a player might strike out 200 times and receive little criticism, as long as he's also hitting home runs.

And can one compare any players from before and after 1947? That was the year Jackie Robinson broke the color barrier. Before then, MLB had shamefully barred black players. The best black, Hispanic, and Asian players had to compete

WHERE WERE THEIR GLOVES?

One unusual difference between baseball eras is that players used to leave their gloves on the field after the third out of each inning. Some dropped them in foul grounds. Center fielders, shortstops, and second basemen tossed theirs into the outfield. Then they all picked up their gloves again when they returned to play defense. A rule change in 1953 forced players to take their gloves into the dugout.

in other leagues. That meant no major league player truly competed against the best players in the world until at least 40 years later, when an influx of Hispanic and Asian players fully integrated the major leagues.

Is comparing players from different eras like comparing apples and oranges? Some believe it can be done. Boston Red Sox Hall of Famer Ted Williams hit .406 in 1941. He was the last hitter with a .400 batting average over a full season. But could he do it while facing pitchers who throw the nasty array of pitches common today? And could New York Yankees closer Aroldis Chapman have thrown his fastball 100 miles an hour in the 1920s, given the different training methods of that time?

Nobody knows for sure. But it is certainly fun to think about.

How would Hall of Famer Ted Williams fare against modern pitching?

Ron Blomberg of the New York Yankees was the first MLB player to step to the plate as a designated hitter.

CHAPTER FOUR

THE DH DIFFERENCE

April 6, 1973, was Opening Day across the major leagues. The first game on the American League (AL) slate found the New York Yankees facing their archrivals, the Boston Red Sox, at famous Fenway Park.

The Yankees' Ron Blomberg made history just by stepping up to the plate in the first inning. Blomberg was the first designated hitter (DH) in a major league game.

Many observers believe the DH changed the sport more than any other new rule over the years. The DH bats in place of the pitcher. Great pitchers aren't usually also major league-level hitters. The new rule brought more offense to the game.

There was just one big problem. It was only used in the American League. The National League (NL) refused to change its rules. NL officials argued that the DH removed strategy from the sport. AL managers no longer had to decide if or when to pinch hit for the pitcher.

Most observers did not think the difference between leagues would last. Some felt the American League would drop the DH. Others predicted the National League would adopt it. They figured there was no way the two leagues would continue playing by separate rules.

They figured wrong. Both sides refused to budge. And years after Blomberg stepped to the plate, the DH remains only in the American League.

The differing rules place AL teams at a disadvantage when they play at NL ballparks. Their pitchers must bat in those games. The result is that one of their best hitters must either play in the field or sit on the bench.

Supporters of the DH prefer to watch a top hitter swing the bat rather than a pitcher flailing away at the plate. They argue that baseball is a duller game when pitchers hit. They add that the DH allows aging sluggers to stay active when they are no

David Ortiz took advantage of the DH rule to put together a long and successful career with the Boston Red Sox.

longer strong fielders. Or some DH's are younger players who simply aren't very good fielders. Fans might not have been able to enjoy watching such sluggers as David "Big Papi" Ortiz bash homers for the Boston Red Sox if not for the DH.

But there's no question that the rule changes the strategy of the game. NL managers have to base decisions about removing

EXCELLENT EDGAR

Many consider David Ortiz only the second-best designated hitter ever. Seattle Mariners star Edgar Martinez, like Ortiz, was a DH throughout most of his career. Martinez played 18 seasons and averaged 41 doubles per year while posting a career batting average of .312. He won the AL batting title in 1992 and 1995.

pitchers on more than how they're pitching. They have to consider when it's the pitcher's turn to bat next. NL managers often make "double switches," in which they pull a pitcher and a position player at the same time. Then their replacements swap spots in the batting order to keep the pitcher's spot from coming up soon.

Most baseball experts believe the National League will eventually adopt the DH. On the players' side, most would prefer that because the DH position provides jobs for older players. That gives them all a chance to extend their careers and make more money. But the debate will not end even if the National League adopts the DH. Some fans will lament the change. They believe that strategy is more important to baseball than offense. But would they tell that to Big Papi?

Edgar Martinez was a two-time batting champion who spent the majority of his career as a DH.

Pete Rose holds the MLB record for most career hits, but off-field issues have kept him out of the Hall of Fame.

CHAPTER FIVE

WHO BELONGS IN THE HALL?

It's been said that Pete Rose played baseball like his hair was on fire. His nickname was "Charlie Hustle." He went all out, all the time. He even sprinted to first base after drawing a walk.

The longtime Cincinnati Reds star was one of the greatest hitters to ever wear a major league uniform. He set the all-time career record with 4,256 hits. His 746 doubles rank second in the history of the game. He was named Rookie of the Year in 1963 and NL Most Valuable Player (MVP) in 1973. But Rose is not in the Baseball Hall of Fame.

"Shoeless" Joe Jackson was banned from baseball for his role in the 1919 World Series gambling scandal.

Barry Bonds holds the MLB record for most home runs in a season (73 in 2001) and a career (762 over 22 seasons). Bonds was so feared by opposing pitchers that he led the National League in walks 12 times. He also won seven NL MVP Awards. But Bonds is not in the Hall of Fame.

"Shoeless" Joe Jackson was the Pete Rose of his era. He batted an amazing .408 in 1911 with Cleveland. He averaged 219 hits, 43 doubles, 21 triples, and 34 stolen bases during one three-year period. But Jackson is not in the Hall of Fame.

Why? Each had his own sad story to tell. Rose was banned from baseball for gambling on the sport while he was managing the Reds. Bonds reportedly took steroids to improve his performance. Baseball media who elect Hall members have refused to vote him in. Jackson was among the eight Chicago White Sox players whom gamblers paid to intentionally lose the 1919 World Series. He was banished from the sport forever.

Debates have raged about all three players and others who remain out of the Hall for suspected or proven dirty deeds. Other controversial cases include those of star sluggers Mark McGwire and Sammy Sosa and ace pitcher Roger Clemens. All have been credibly accused of using PEDs.

Any other player with their statistics would be a no-brainer for induction to the Hall. But some believe those players should remain on the outside looking in. After all, some players cheated to improve their numbers. Others, such as Rose and Jackson, gave baseball a black eye by gambling.

Should that matter? One can argue that PED use was common in the late 1990s and early 2000s. One can also claim that MLB was equally to blame. The league ignored, and perhaps even encouraged, the cheating. The sport wanted desperately to turn the page after a nasty labor dispute caused the game to shut down in 1994. The World Series was canceled for the first time ever.

When play resumed, angry fans stayed away from ballparks. It took a historic home run barrage from Bonds, Sosa, McGwire, and others to lure many fans back. Is it possible that MLB officials knew the players were using PEDs but looked the other way? After all, the results were exactly what the league wanted.

Mark McGwire slugged 583 career home runs, but his career statistics are tainted by his emergence during the steroid era.

Others claim that every career statistic achieved by players such as Bonds and Clemens is tainted. They question how many home runs Bonds would have hit, or how many batters Clemens would have struck out, if they had not been using PEDs.

Many fans and even media members do not recognize the career home run record Bonds set. They claim it still belongs to Hank Aaron, who hit 755 homers, presumably without illegal enhancement. People who think Bonds isn't the legitimate home run king usually also want him banned from the Hall.

But there is another side to the story. It can be argued that Bonds gained Hall of Fame credentials before the steroid era. He had already won three NL MVP Awards in the early 1990s. His on-base percentage exceeded .400 every year from 1990 to 1998. He won eight Gold Glove Awards during that time for defensive brilliance.

A similar argument could be made for Clemens, who made his debut with the Red Sox in 1984. Over the next 13 years, the hard-throwing right-hander won three AL Cy Young Awards. He also was the AL MVP in 1986, when he led Boston to the World Series. But questions about Clemens arose after a suspicious late-career resurgence. He won the Cy Young Award

Roger Clemens and other pitchers were suspected of using PEDs to throw harder.

INCHING CLOSER TO COOPERSTOWN

Players must earn 75 percent of the ballots to be voted into the Baseball Hall of Fame. Barry Bonds and Roger Clemens were getting closer in 2017. Both received 54 percent of the vote. That marked a rise of almost 10 percent over 2016. But it still meant that nearly half of the voters believed their alleged steroid use should keep them out of the Hall.

four more times after age 34, a period when most power pitchers are no longer able to dominate opposing batters.

Supporters of Bonds and Clemens claim that every player should be judged based on his era. The two tainted stars rose above other alleged steroid users to become the best hitter and pitcher of their generation.

But was it a level playing field? Many other players did not cheat. And that stains the achievements of Bonds, Sosa, Clemens, and others who took PEDs to gain an unfair advantage.

Those on both sides of the argument must agree to disagree. It will be up to the voters to decide whether any or all of those players will someday be enshrined into the Baseball Hall of Fame.

Fans of Bonds argue that he put together Hall of Fame numbers before he was suspected of using PEDs.

TOPICS FOR FURTHER DISCUSSION

- Will any player ever hit .400 over the course of a full season again?

- Should MLB limit the number of relief pitchers a team can use in a game?

- What can be done to attract more African-American athletes to the sport of baseball?

- Is the fact that batters are striking out an average of once an inning bad for the sport?

- Is the strike zone as called by major league umpires too low?

- Are replay challenges good for the sport, even though they add length to already long games?

- Should relief pitchers be limited to three warmups when they enter a game to save time?

- Who is the greatest pitcher of all time?

- What is the hardest position to play?